How Big Government Won the West

Stephen J. Rockwell

St. Joseph's College, New York

In class recently, a student suggested that the American people were better off in the nineteenth century, when government regulation and activity had not yet interfered with the force and freedom of independent entrepreneurs. She mentioned the railroads, and how great tycoons ran lines across the continent, built great works, and achieved great things.

I asked her where the railroads got the land from.

She didn't have an answer. After a few moments, a different student raised his hand and said, "The Indians?"

"Good. How?" I asked.

Silence.

"Didn't we just kill them?" one student finally volunteered.

"Who killed them?"

"The Army?"

"OK. Is that all we did? Kill Indians and move onto their land?"

At this point, the class was stumped. We lack a general narrative for what happened before U.S. citizens and companies came to possess and then build upon the land; we lack a narrative for exactly how the continent was conquered.

One reason we lack these deeper explanations is the continuing appeal of a narrative of inevitability—a sparsely populated continent, occupied by a few doomed savages, was (of course) eventually settled by industrious, aggressive, and successful go-getters. It was actually pretty easy, aside from fights with bears and treks across frozen mountains.

But this popular narrative has always obscured the fundamentally important, and *active*, role of the federal government in the nation's first century. The federal government got the land from the Indians, through treaties, administration, and war, and only then parceled it out to land companies, states, speculators, and railroads. The federal government set itself up, in law and in practice, as the essential middleman in all—ALL—land acquisitions from Indians. Only through the activity of the federal government could land acquisition and westward expansion take place.

Thinking of westward expansion and economic growth as somehow taking place without the federal government, in a land of individual and entrepreneurial freedom, is simply wrong. But until we ask where the land came from, and *how* we got it, we may never see the very visible hand of government regulation and activity in the nation's first century. Big government won the West. Recognizing this fact alters the meta-narrative of American history, and blows up our most cherished myths.

$\mathbf{T}$ake the Louisiana Purchase as an example. Most Americans think of this signal event in U.S. continental expansion as a pretty straightforward thing. President Thomas Jefferson grabs his ridiculous quill pen and signs a deal with hard-up France, buying vast regions in North America for a piddling fifteen million dollars. Done. If any further discussion takes place, it usually focuses on the constitutionality of the deal, and the implications of such a transaction for the development of presidential powers under the Constitution.

Historians like James Loewen, though, estimate that the actual cost to the United States of the lands involved in the Louisiana Purchase was closer to *three hundred million dollars*, not fifteen million. This is because what Jefferson actually bought from France was, effectively, the right to acquire the land from its inhabitants— thousands and thousands of American Indians, in hundreds of different and distinct Indian tribes and nations, who were already living on it. The United States, having bought out France's rights, still had to buy the land from the people occupying it.

At the center of the land acquisition and distribution process, before and after the Louisiana Purchase, sat the federal government. Beginning in the 1790s, the federal government established itself as an indispensable piece of the puzzle: under the Trade and Intercourse Acts of 1790, all land acquired from Indians had to be obtained at a public treaty involving the federal government; all other acquisitions were void. This and other federal laws and regulations controlled the land acquisition process through the nineteenth century. In New York alone, the necessity of federal involvement still drives current issues like the Oneida Indian Nation's claims to lands in upstate New York, and the Shinnecock Indians' claims on Long Island. In both cases, the absence of the federal government's participation in land transfers more than a hundred years ago anchors the Indians' legal arguments today.

Treaties were not always nice administrative processes, of course. The U.S. cheated, capitalizing on languages, concepts, and clauses poorly understood by Indian negotiators. The U.S. also made habits of getting Indians drunk before they signed, and of bribing translators to lie about what the treaties meant; the government often unilaterally changed treaty provisions in the U.S.'s favor before ratification; and, when it helped the U.S., treaty commissioners signed treaties with illegitimate rump elements and passed them off as the will of entire native communities.

But this is, in important ways, another story. The story here is the indispensable, intrusive, and active role played by the federal government. People, companies, and states couldn't get land without the federal government's involvement, and so the federal government in the nineteenth century was a player. When we start the nation's narrative with "settlers" building cabins, or with railroads binding the continent together, we see only the entrepreneurs. We miss what happened before; we miss the careful and organized establishment, by government, of the conditions that made such growth possible in the first place.

When small-government, free-market advocates tout the gains made by early American entrepreneurs, they ignore the many ways in which the federal government regulated and shaped the early economy that they lionize. The tariff, for example, dominated trading relations and protected American domestic manufactures into the twentieth century; it was an essentially protectionist economy, not a "free" one, that built the country in the nineteenth century. Aside from the tariff, the feds controlled some economic sectors, like land acquisition, and they regulated others, such as trade in alcohol and weapons. The federal government even competed with private business, a fact that becomes increasingly relevant as Americans press for a public health care option, or for Medicare-for-all. The federal government competed directly in the critically important fur trade as early as the Washington Administration. The Founding Fathers themselves built the first regulatory schemes, the first administrative bureaucracies, and the first examples of federal competition with private businesses.

Blame George Washington. In his annual addresses in 1793 and 1794, the leader of the founding generation exhorted Congress to establish a system of government-run trading houses, called factories. Congress appropriated $500,000 in 1795 for the construction of government factories, and it formally authorized the plan in 1796. By 1807 the system was being run by the War Department's John Mason, the son of founding father George Mason. The not-for-profit factories operated at key points along the nation's frontier, including points in the South, the Old Northwest, and eventually Green Bay, Detroit, and Chicago.

Intentionally underselling private companies and independent traders, the factories aimed to limit the influence of unscrupulous independent traders and drive the lucrative fur trade into the hands of the government or into the hands of large, responsible companies like John Jacob Astor's American Fur Company. Astor's interests blossomed; independent traders quit the field, unable to pay the bonds and secure the licenses that the government mandated for legal entry into the trade. The government made winners of the large companies and losers of independent businessmen, by competing directly in the fur trade.

The government's rationale was simple: it was trying to avoid costly and unpredictable conflicts with the Indians. The factories were never designed to be moneymakers. Instead, they gave the federal government a presence on the frontier and a foothold in business, allowing federal agents to limit the impact of independent traders—impacts that political leaders at the national level feared might spark an Indian war, which in turn could invite European powers back into armed conflict with the United States.

The factories also aided the land acquisition process, as part of a sophisticated, integrated government policy. In a revealing 1803 letter to Indiana Territorial Governor William Henry Harrison, President Thomas Jefferson—the patron saint of limited government and the architect of the $300M project to buy the West from Indians—revealed the federal government's operating scheme for how big government would win the West:

> When they [Indians] withdraw
> themselves to the culture of a small piece
> of land, they will perceive how useless to
> them are their extensive forests, and will
> be willing to pare them off from time to
> time in exchange for necessaries for their

farms and families. To promote this disposition to exchange lands, which they have to spare and we want, for necessaries, which we have to spare and they want, we shall push our trading houses, and be glad to see the good and influential individuals among them run in debt, because we observe that when these debts get beyond what the individuals can pay, they become willing to lop them off by a cession of lands.

At our trading houses, too, we mean to sell so low as merely to repay us cost and charges, so as neither to lessen nor enlarge our capital. This is what private traders cannot do, for they must gain; they will consequently retire from the competition, and we shall thus get clear of this pest without giving offence or umbrage to the Indians. In this way our settlements will gradually circumscribe and approach the Indians, and they will in time either incorporate with us as citizens of the United States, or remove beyond the Mississippi.

Much of the point for us is in recognizing the critical role of the federal government in the nineteenth century, mandating policies to manage continental expansion. Government bureaucrats and regulators ran the show on the ground then, just as they do today. The factory system ran for decades, against growing opposition from western traders and from successful major corporations—corporations like Astor's that owed their successes to the federal government's program in the first place. Agents in the War Department and the Office of Indian Trade did the fieldwork of operating the factory system, storing and shipping furs, supplying and negotiating treaties, authorizing licenses, taking bonds, adjudicating disputes, and designing adaptations to policy and administration.

And lest we marginalize Indian affairs as a sidelight to the "mainstream" of American history, let's remember that George Washington, Andrew Jackson, and William Henry Harrison all rode to the presidency on careers fired in Indian affairs. Winfield Scott, Lewis Cass, and others throughout the nineteenth century came close. Abraham Lincoln, Jefferson Davis, Ulysses S. Grant, and James Garfield all spent time in their early careers dealing with issues related to Indian affairs and westward expansion. Astor became the country's richest man thanks to Indian labor and government regulation in the fur trade. Indians and expansion were central issues as the prominent government presence started to sweep across the continent, and across the century.

Today, national parks and historic sites chart the nineteenth century federal government's presence, if only you look for it. One summer, while in Boston to see the Yankees beat the Red Sox, a friend and I took a launch from the waterfront out to the Harbor Islands. A stormy, rainy day nixed any hiking, but the installations and fortifications being restored there bear witness to the heavy role played by government and the defense industry as early as the 1810s and 1820s. The U.S. established the Bernard Board in 1816, headed by Napoleon's former aide-de-camp, Simon Bernard. The Board aimed to design a series of seacoast fortifications, including Fort Warren on Georges Island, that would deter and, if necessary, help repel any future invasions. So effective in the deterrence, they were never used to fight—and thus their importance and effectiveness have been largely forgotten.

The Harbor Island batteries were one link in a chain of coastal fortifications—again, rarely used, and thus rarely remembered—that stretches from Maine to Florida, into the Gulf Coast, and all the way to California. Fort Knox in Maine—which also features the world's second-tallest bridge-based observation deck, atop the Penobscot Narrows Bridge—on a recent summer's day featured children playing pirate, history buffs examining cannons, and a full parking lot. It's a cool fort. But only the detailed, oft-overlooked displays reveal the coordinated role of the installation in national defense and the government's role in supplying the town with years of construction jobs. Fort Sumter, Baltimore's Fort McHenry, Fort Adams near Newport, Rhode Island, Virginia's Fortress Monroe, and San Francisco's Fort Winfield Scott (at the Presidio) are among the fortifications constructed in this decades-long effort. The list also includes Fort Schuyler, now part of the SUNY Maritime College in New York, near the Throgs Neck Bridge, and Fort Pulaski on Cockspur Island, Georgia.

Go west, and you'll come across the same kinds of chains, only this time they're land-locked. The U.S. constructed lines of forts from North to South, designed to protect Americans from Europeans and Indians and to facilitate management and control as the nation expanded westward. One line stretched from Fort Snelling, on the Mississippi River near Minneapolis, to places like Fort Leavenworth and Fort Scott in Kansas, and on to Fort Smith in Arkansas. Another tied together the West Coast in the 1840s and 1850s, at places like Fort Walla Walla, Fort Humboldt, and Fort Tejon. Other chains extended East-West, including places like Fort Larned and Fort Dodge on the Santa Fe Trail, and Fort Kearny, Fort Laramie, and Fort Hall on the Oregon Trail.

Look deeper, and even more engaging remnants of the nineteenth century's government presence appear. One of my favorites is Fort Gibson in Oklahoma—the end point for so many Indian nations' trails of tears. At

Fort Gibson, Indians forcibly removed from the east were held and processed, then scattered to their new homes and communities in the Indian Territory. Years later, whites would see the Indian Territory as a giant, government-created roadblock to western expansion. Today at the site, barely any mention is made of its central role in one of America's signal tragedies—it just looks like a sleepy, empty old fort by the railroad tracks.

900 miles from Fort Gibson, in Zanesville, Ohio, stands the National Road Museum. Paired in the same building with a museum honoring local hero Zane Grey, the National Road Museum features a giant 3-D diorama snaking along the museum's walls, from one huge room to the next, depicting, in true scale modeling expertise, the development of the National Road from 1806 (Jefferson again!) to the twentieth century. A government-instituted, publicly funded, contractor-constructed, and government-managed effort to link east and west, encourage economic development, and spur western settlement, the Road is a critical part of the nineteenth-century United States' story. Archer Butler Hulbert sang its praises in 1901:

> When this west was in its teens and began suddenly outstripping itself, to the marvel of the world, one of the momentous factors in its progress was the building of a great National Road, from

the Potomac river to the Mississippi river, by the United States Government—a highway seven hundred miles in length, at a cost of seven millions of treasure. This ribbon of road, winding its way through Maryland, Pennsylvania, Ohio, Indiana and Illinois, toward the Mississippi, was one of the most important steps in that movement of national expansion which followed the conquest of the west. It is probably impossible for us to realize fully what it meant to this west when that vanguard of surveyors came down the western slopes of the Alleghanies, hewing a thoroughfare which should, in one generation, bind distant and half-acquainted states together in bonds of common interest, sympathy and ambition...[The National Road] proved that a republic of loyal people could scorn the old European theory that mountains are imperative boundaries of empire.

Such shadows of the big, active government of the nineteenth century blanket the nation. The federal government built post roads and military roads in Florida and Tennessee, protected commercial routes like the Santa Fe Trail, and regulated the great population migrations across the Great Platte River Road, better known as the Oregon Trail. Government activity sparked and located what are now major cities, like Fort Wayne, Fort Dearborn (now Chicago), and Fort Washington (now Cincinnati). Government funds built lighthouses on the Great Lakes and led a great Pacific expedition in the 1840s; government soldiers protected mining interests against labor disruptions as far north as Copper Harbor, at the top of Michigan's Upper Peninsula, they occupied cities as far south as Mexico City, and they protected railroaders and workers and owners as they built lines and mines across the Great Plains and into the Rockies.

The government's involvement runs all the way to the west coast, right into the lobby of the U.S. Grant Hotel in San Diego. This majestic hotel in downtown San Diego is a living reminder of President Grant's 1875 executive order that reserved a landbase for the Kumayaay Indians of southern California. Thanks in great part to Grant's action, the Kumayaay survived—and, flush with casino revenue, in the 1990s they bought and restored the crumbling, once-grand Grant and restored it to glory. Displays in the U.S. Grant's lobby commemorate the difference big government made in the community's life over a century ago.

Seduced by a narrative of individualized settlement and an entrepreneurial, free-market heritage, we fail to see these kinds of historical sites in context with each other. Together, these sites reveal a continental grid of

16

North-South defense lines and East-West commerce and migration lines, directed and managed by government activity in defense, infrastructure, and commercial development. The feds regularly impacted economic activity, picked winners and losers, and provided jobs and resources, as government agents and officials managed expansion and settlement.

J. W. Bean may have been surprised to see a federal agent on his doorstep in St. Michael, on the far west coast of Alaska, in 1873. The agent was there to investigate whether or not Bean was violating federal liquor laws by manufacturing and selling liquor to Indians and Eskimos. Special Indian Agent Frederick S. Hall investigated Bean, Ivan Kashevnikoff, and other men in the distant regions of Alaska, reporting back to the Federal District Attorney in Portland, Oregon. And even though the government had trouble trying to police the alcohol trade in Alaska in the closing quarter of the nineteenth century, there was the federal agent, trudging through the snow, searching houses, and confiscating whiskey.

Years earlier, in 1831, Congress had made it a crime to cut and remove timber from public lands. In 1854, according to historian Lucile Kane, a man in Wisconsin confronted a timber agent on the Manistee River. "When …[the agent] came to seize my lumber," the man reported, "I told him that I had lived under 3 Kings reign and a part of a Queens reign and I never [did] see property sized [sic] and taken away from poor people as they did from us." The man asked if he could appeal to any authority higher than the timber agent, but "the agent answered that there was no one higher than he except God Almighty."

Years earlier still, white settlers attacked Cherokee Indians in the Tennessee region, on land that still belonged to the Cherokees. The attackers actually shot bullets through their own clothes, to establish a self-defense claim should they be prosecuted by the federal government for violating the boundaries established by federal treaty. These folks knew that intruding on the Indians' unceded lands was likely to get them in trouble with federal agents for trespassing, and they were already anticipating their legal defense in federal court. This was in 1796.

Each of these cases, representing a broad range of eras and locations, exposes the visible role of federal regulators and federal regulations in eighteenth- and nineteenth-century America. The federal government was a player pretty much everywhere, and even the Great got caught in its net: Indian agent Silas Dinsmoor once detained a group of Andrew Jackson's slaves, who were being moved along the Natchez Trace (and through the agent's jurisdiction) without the proper passports and paperwork. Federal rules regulated arms and weapons sales in Indian country, federal licenses were needed to carry on the fur trade, passports were needed for travel, federal commissions adjudicated disputes over land titles, federal agents quarantined sailors coming from abroad with diseases, federal agents collected taxes and tariffs, federal agents prosecuted violators of the Fugitive Slave Act, federal judges extended federal jurisdiction to frontier areas.

Government action impacted larger communities, as well. In the early 1790s, when the West was in Pennsylvania, anti-government activists in the western part of the state found themselves confronted by a 12,000-man fighting force led by perennial victor George Washington. The rebels, upset at an excise tax on whiskey, had decided that they wouldn't pay it. Washington and the visible hand made sure to quash the threat that they posed to the legitimacy of the new constitutional government. Before the rebellion dissipated, though, harassment of federal agents—threats, barn burnings, tar and featherings, burnings in effigy—had spread throughout the region. The threat was real; the smackdown was quick and efficient.

History tends to take note of the Whiskey Rebellion, but usually as a study in the early application of presidential power. Because we *like* Washington and a strong presidency, the government's effectiveness is seen as a good thing. And because we like the Constitution and the confederation of the original colonies, the action overall is seen as a milestone on the path toward national unification. But what we miss is the application of big government—force and strength and dominance—over some of the same individual rebels who had, just a few years before, fought to overthrow the tyranny of England. As local historian Ned Frear writes,

> Alexander Hamilton had managed the enactment of an excise tax on whiskey. In country where you could find a steaming still down every tenth lane, the tax was an outrageous, unfair blow to a man's liberty. And when a farmer could be hauled to Philadelphia for court, kept for weeks, obliged to pay expensive lawyers while he was losing all his income at home, it was ruinous. And now, the national government, in Philadelphia, was raising a militia to come make war on the people who had a legitimate grievance. It was too much.

In the 1790s, in the west of Pennsylvania—and in the South in the 1830s, in Wisconsin in the 1850s, and in Alaska in the 1870s—people resisted what they perceived as the heavy hand of big government tyranny.

The pre-Civil War South *loved* big government.

In June of 1854, fifteen thousand soldiers marched Anthony Burns through the streets of Boston and onto a U.S. revenue cutter docked in Boston Harbor. Burns had escaped from slavery in Virginia, only to be recaptured in Boston. As Burns became a visible victim of 1850's Fugitive Slave Act, forcibly returned to slavery by the federal government, fifty thousand people lined the streets of Boston to watch the procession. Twenty years earlier, big government was satisfying aggressive southern interests by ethnically cleansing American Indians from the region. U.S. troops identified, collected, and removed Indians to the West by force, where they would live on lands administered by a federal government that assumed vast powers. Slavery and Indian affairs are two of the most prominent, and least recognized, applications of big government in the nineteenth century.

When we think of slavery as a states' rights issue, we sometimes forget that the Constitution's three-fifths compromise cemented slavery at the foundation of the republic, rewarding slave states with greater representation in Congress as they enslaved more people. The Constitution's property rights protections also obligated the federal government to protect rights in slaves. Perhaps the most notorious application of such power over people's lives was the Fugitive Slave Act of

1850, which authorized federal agents to force citizens to aid slave-catching efforts. The law effectively nullified state laws like New York's personal liberty laws, and the mere presence of the Act terrorized black communities and infringed sharply even on white ones. Actual enforcement of the Act led to high-tension conflicts between citizens and the federal government, such as the return of Anthony Burns and the seizure of James Hamlet in New York City.

The feds were strong sometimes on the other side, too. After the federal government outlawed the importation of slaves in 1808, the Navy patrolled the coasts of Africa and the United States looking for violators. President John Quincy Adams negotiated an agreement with England that allowed British naval personnel to board American ships to search for slaves—and this was *after* the War of 1812, which had been sparked in part by British boardings of American ships. Citizens monitored the intricate involvement of federal officials in disputes taking place in territories like Kansas, as local supporters and opponents of slavery clashed amid the active role being played by territorial governors appointed by President Franklin Pierce. Federal courts—most notably in the *Dred Scott* and *Plessy v. Ferguson* decisions—reinforced slavery and Jim Crow throughout the era.

As the federal government was a player in slavery and its events, so too was it a player on the ground in

Indian affairs. Consider this description of the Potawatomis' removal from Indiana, written by a priest who witnessed the event and who is quoted in Grant Foreman's classic account, *The Last Trek of the Indians*:

On September 4, 1838, they were lined up, some afoot, some on ponies, followed by the wagons, and all heavily guarded with guards at the rear with bayonets, which were often used to keep the weak ones in the procession. Before starting the torch was applied to their village, so that they might see their homes destroyed and they would not want to return. When all was in readiness, this grewsome procession, nearly three miles long, like a funeral procession, which in reality it was, started on its final journey. It was a very sickly season...

[The order of march was] The United States flag, carried by a dragoon; then one of the principal officers, next the staff baggage carts, then the carriage, which during the whole trip was kept for the use of the Indian chiefs; then one or two chiefs on horseback led a line of 250 or 300 horses ridden by men, women and children in single file, after the manner of savages. On the flanks of the line at equal distance from each other were the dragoons and volunteers, hastening the stragglers, often with severe gestures and bitter words. After this cavalry came a file of forty baggage wagons filled with luggage and Indians. The sick were lying in them, rudely jolted, under a canvas which, far from protecting them from the dust and heat, only deprived them of air, for they were as if buried under this burning canopy—several died thus[.]

Such is not the result of a weak, disorganized, and bungling government. Such is the result of a clear and accepted administrative mission, careful preparation, logistical planning, and execution.

While we sometimes remember Indian removal, we have almost no remembered narrative at all of the U.S. military removing American squatters from unceded Indian lands. Taught that the federal government was small, and powerless to control the unruly roughnecks on the frontier, we're encouraged to excuse the problems surrounding encroachments on Indian land. We're encouraged to think that the government was powerless to stop or even shape the inevitable spread of white settlement, and the accompanying destruction of native communities. But the government *did* police those borders. Federal troops removed white squatters from Cherokee lands, for example, in 1797-98, 1803, 1804, 1805, 1808, 1809, and 1810. The action in 1797 involved 1200 soldiers, who removed intruders, burned cabins, and wrecked fences. In the 1820s, President John Quincy Adams positioned federal troops between the Creek Nation and Georgians threatening to trespass into Indian territory guaranteed by federal treaty—a move that risked civil war and a great clash of federal and state sovereignty. In 1832, U.S. troops from Fort Mitchell burned the town of Irwinton, where white squatters had illegally entered Creek lands and established a community. The soldiers burned cabins, broke fences, and forced the intruders out of the Creek Nation and back to the United States. It was under President Andrew Jackson, in the middle of his aggressive push for Indian removal, that the military burned Irwinton.

These situations caused great conflict and consternation, and the nineteenth century witnessed no shortage of retaliation against federal agents. Along with extra-judicial efforts that echoed the actions of the whiskey rebels, the era saw military officers put on trial for their actions upholding federal mandates. County officials in Alabama, for example, brought charges against the federal officers behind the burning of Irwinton. Alabama investigated and charged General John Wool for his actions in Indian affairs— Wool often found himself acting on behalf of the Indians, to uphold federal commitments and preeminence against the actions of states and white squatters. Captain Archibald Turk was tried by Georgia for murder, after white intruders died being removed by Turk's troops from Cherokee lands.

At the heart of these kinds of collisions during Indian removal lay a debate over the *purposes* of the exercise of federal power. Southern state leaders and inhabitants weren't anti-federal-government, and they certainly weren't small government advocates—they wanted the federal government to be active and strong, in order to remove Indians. When the feds upheld federal treaties and federal control of land and managed expansion, then the South complained about big government. Not because it was big, but because it was doing the wrong thing. Once big government under President Andrew Jackson retasked the military to the identifying, imprisoning, and removing of entire Indian communities, the South was much more satisfied. The pre-Civil War South loved an active federal government when it served southern regional interests in slavery and Indian affairs.

Nations are not built and bound together solely by infrastructure, technology, and conquest. The social contract must bind together the people's hearts and minds—their commitment to seeing each other as

26

members of the same community, linked by love and concern and interest. Social ties are as much a part of winning the West and unifying the continent as are the harder targets of government action.

Support, protection, and relief offered to our fellow citizens—social policy—is a big part of today's debate over big government. Whether it's welfare, health care, student loans, veterans' benefits, or 9/11 victims' compensation, we debate the appropriate role of government in protecting and empowering its citizens (and others). Advocates of government action see efforts to improve people's lives, to take care of people in need, to rectify injustice. Others see the heavy hand of government as a force for waste, fraud, and abuse; a force that saps individual will and responsibility; a force that threatens our freedom.

Ron Paul, for example, who professes a deep allegiance to our founding ideals and to the notion of a limited, carefully circumscribed role for the federal government, has argued that the feds should probably not be involved in disaster relief. While allowing for some role by state governments or by the feds for rescue operations, Paul has criticized FEMA and called disaster relief efforts at the federal level "bad constitutional law." Yet Paul, like most folks who have internalized an image of the early federal government as small, limited, and narrowly constrained in its activity, seems unaware of the very early precedents set by the founding generation—

the guys who *wrote* the Constitution—in social policy. As social historian Michele Landis writes in the Northwestern University Law Review,

> The key to understanding both historical and contemporary patterns of American social welfare legislation, policy, spending, and jurisprudence is found not in the New Deal, nor even in the system of pensions adopted following the Civil War. Rather, the origin of the American welfare state is found in the narratives of blame and fate that surfaced originally in eighteenth- and early nineteenth-century contests over 'disaster' relief...[D]uring the period from 1789 to 1874, the Constitution provided no serious impediment to the development of disaster relief into the first sustained, organized social welfare program of the federal government.

Landis notes that President James Madison— perhaps the very definition of a "founding father" when it comes to the meaning of the Constitution—signed relief bills appropriating millions of dollars in cash assistance, food and clothing distributions, and property indemnifications. The provision of disaster relief by the

28

federal government thus goes back to the nation's roots, fully realized and sanctioned by the founding generation itself. And the public was on board: according to administrative law scholar Jerry Mashaw, citizens submitted to Congress, in its first twelve years, nearly three thousand petitions for "relief of some sort"—whether disaster relief, relief from "fire, flood, or seizure by pirates", or seemingly anything else people could think of.

As another example of how our current discussions ache from a lack of historical awareness, I remember numerous discussions taking place after 9/11 over whether or not the federal government—as an expression of the national community—should compensate that event's victims. Some argued that sympathy and the nature of a military attack justified, even required, that our representatives help alleviate the suffering of our fellow citizens. Others argued that it was not the role of the federal government to compensate or indemnify citizens who were, after all, going about their ordinary business. They have their own insurance, that argument went, and people need to take care of themselves.

The debate often approached the issue as though the government had never helped its citizens following an attack, as though we'd never faced this kind of situation before. But the federal government indemnified U.S. settlers in newly ceded areas of the U.S. frontier against Indian depredations as early as the 1790s. Federal agents took claims from white settlers, and federal officials decided whether or not the national government would compensate people for their losses. Thousands of people submitted claims for reimbursement from the federal government for depredations allegedly committed by Indians, and an entire administrative process was established to organize and adjudicate them. Some cases dragged on for decades, eventually being settled by children and grandchildren. While the federal government usually opted not to pay—no surprise there—the fact of a policy and of an administrative process run by federal agents was a central part of the expansion experience.

The legacies of the federal government's social policy endeavors in the nineteenth century are certainly less visible than the fortifications, roads, lighthouses, and towns. Still, they were—and are—relevant. The nation set up programs to help Indians, usually as payment for the lands ceded by the tribes, including education guarantees, health care and vaccinations, religious instruction, vocational training, housing, and economic development. But the U.S. also assisted revolutionary war veterans with pensions and land bounties, marking some of the first social programs targeted at citizens and veterans. The federal government in the nineteenth century provided widows' and mothers' pensions, and veterans' disability pensions. The role of the feds in health care goes back at least as far as the 1798 act that created the Federal Marine Hospital System, which served seamen at a system of facilities located in the nation's harbors and ports. The 1862 Homestead Act helped millions of Americans buy land in the West. The list goes on.

In other areas, federal activity worked to build and bind communities into a nation; leaders knew that wouldn't happen by itself. The historian Richard John has demonstrated how the early Post Office built roads and linked communities in a nation-building exercise that bound west to east and subsidized not only newspapers and communications, but stagecoaches, inns, and contractors who surveyed and did other works. Federal posts like Fort Kearney, on the Oregon Trail in Nebraska, were welcome landmarks along the journey, providing free public services and some degree of order and protection—not even so much from Indians, but from the private traders along the route, whose reputations for unfair dealings and price gouging were legendary. Federal expeditionary missions, like those of Lewis & Clark, John Fremont, and Zebulon Pike, federal efforts like the 1850s' continental railroad surveys, and federal protection for Americans traveling abroad, through ambassadors and naval stations, all worked to build the early social network through big, active government.

So how did all of this get done? Treaties, factory systems, Indian removal, timber regulation, military supply, vaccination programs, education benefits, road

31

construction, railroad subsidies, veterans' pensions—to return to my question to the students, How did it happen?

It happened with what we today call big government. The key is to recognize westward expansion across the continent as the result of public policy—the first great national endeavor, planned, managed, and executed by the strong and influential hand of government. And finding it in the nineteenth century demonstrates decisively that big government is hardly the creation of Franklin Roosevelt and the New Deal Democrats, johnny-come-latelies entering the scene midway through to steal our freedoms and yoke us to a powerful central state. Big government, in fact, is the creation of the founding generation— not potential, but actually built at the start.

"Big government" usually lacks definition—we see it as a conglomeration of things, and we use the term as something we all understand so clearly that it doesn't need a definition. But defining it certainly helps us see it in the nineteenth century.

When people complain about big government, they're usually complaining about big, expensive things being done, run by distant and unaccountable officials, over whom we have very little control—even though what's being done seems to affect us on a day-to-day level. And so big government can be thought of as a combination of three elements: national programs and policies; bureaucratic structures and personnel to design and administer those programs, often in conflict with the desires and demands of some citizens and elected leaders; and intrusiveness, that sense we have that we are not totally free and independent individuals. So understood, big government won the West and characterized American life in the nineteenth century.

Once we ask where the land came from, and how we got it, we see this in play in myriad ways. The whiskey rebels, the squatters on unceded Indians lands who fired through their own clothes, and the guy with the still in Alaska confronted the agents of big government directly, across the nation's farthest frontiers. The Indians forcibly removed from their homes across the continent, and the whites moving in; the men, women, and children held as property, and the slaves captured and returned to their owners; the investors reaping the rewards of corporate profit and patent protection and federal judicial process—all of these felt the touch of big government.

Armies of civil servants and soldiers moved across the landscape in the nineteenth century, operating with vast grants of discretionary authority, in bureaucratic agencies like the War Department, the Bureau of Indian Affairs, the General Land Office, and the U.S. Corps of Topographical Engineers. They often operated against the wishes of elected leaders and democratic majorities, adding that essentially frustrating element of big government which often confronts us today. Federal agents set up Indian reservations in California, despite whites who wanted the feds to remove the Indians out of the state. The government selected certain roads and railroad routes over others; fur trade regulations and the tariff benefited some industries and hurt others. The Freedmen's Bureau and the military protected the civil rights of newly freed slaves after the Civil War. Each of these examples, and countless others, witnessed federal agents making decisions opposed by *someone*.

This is never to suggest that big government is an unqualified good. Big government in the nineteenth century helped grow a great economy, but it also enforced slavery and dispossessed hundreds of thousands of American Indians. Further, it abused and demoralized many of these populations—by design. It had many of the same horrible effects that worry sincere opponents of big government today, like Ron Paul and Paul Ryan. Where Ron Paul and others go wrong is in arguing that big government is a new thing, anathema to the founders' vision and poison to our storied past. Love him or hate him, George W. Bush talked about smaller government but responded to public crises with bigger government: the Department of Homeland Security, the Wall Street bailout, a worldwide prison system, even No Child Left Behind. Barack Obama's visions for health care, infrastructure development, business subsidy, voting rights enforcement, and the use of drones and extrajudicial killings, run along the same lines. The big government instincts of Bush and Obama are the modern manifestations of a big government DNA, a genetic line that tracks back directly to the founders themselves—to Washington, Hamilton, and even Jefferson.

The founders built big government. The trick now—as it was then—is to limit its potential for disaster and harm, and lead it towards good and responsible ends. We can do that best by retiring the talking points about how the Constitution and big government are somehow antithetical. That's a catchy abstract debate, but it completely misses the history, and the present, of actual governance.